United States Air Force

ELLEN HOPKINS

Heinemann Library
Chicago, Illinois

© 2004 Heinemann Library
a division of Reed Elsevier, Inc.
Chicago, Illinois

Customer Service 888-454-2279

Visit our website at www.heinemannlibrary.com

Designed by Herman Adler Design
Photo research by Bill Broyles
Printed and bound in the United States by Lake Book Manufacturing, Inc.

08 07 06 05
10 9 8 7 6 5 4 3 2

Library of Congress Cataloging-in-Publication Data
Hopkins, Ellen.
  Know it! United States Air Force / by Ellen Hopkins.
    p. cm.
Summary: Provides an overview of the United States Air Force, including its history, weapons, and vehicles.
Includes bibliographical references and index.
  ISBN 1-4034-0187-X (HC), 1-4034-0444-5 (Pbk.)
  1. United States. Air Force--Juvenile literature. [1. United States. Air Force.] I. Title.
  UG633 .H6273 2003
  358.4'00973--dc21

2002015400

Acknowledgments
The author and publisher are grateful to the following for permission to reproduce copyright material:
Cover courtesy of the United States Air Force
Title page, pp. 4, 5T, 12, 16, 17, 18, 19, 20R, 21, 22, 24, 25, 26, 28, 30, 31, 34, 36, 37, 38, 43 Department of Defense; p. 5B Reuters NewMedia Inc./Corbis; pp. 6, 7, 20L, 27, 29, 32, 33, 39, 44, 45 United States Air Force; p. 8 Hulton Archive/Getty Images; p. 9 Bettmann/Corbis; p.10 John Fleck; p. 11 National Archives and Records Administration; pp. 13, 14, 15T Bettmann/Corbis; p. 15B Boeing Management Company; p. 23 Corbis; pp. 40, 41 United States Air Force/Getty Images; p. 42 Nati Harnik/AP Wide World Photos

Special thanks to Lt. Col. G.A. Lofaro for his review of this book.

Every effort has been made to contact copyright holders of any material reproduced in this book. Any omissions will be rectified in subsequent printings if notice is given to the publisher.

Note to the Reader: Some words are shown in bold, **like this.** You can find out what they mean by looking in the glossary.

Contents

Through Aerospace Power

*On September the 11th, enemies of freedom committed an act of war against our country... Americans have known surprise attacks—but never before on thousands of **civilians**. All of this was brought upon us in a single day—and night fell on a different world, a world where freedom itself is under attack.*

President George W. Bush

The United States of America was not prepared for the **terrorist** attacks on the World Trade Center in New York and the Pentagon in Washington, D.C. Yet within minutes, Air National Guard fighter jets roared into action. Part of the United States Air Force, they help defend the United States.

President Bush and Secretary of Defense Rumsfeld look at the Pentagon on September 12, 2001.

An F-16 in flight. In 1991, during Operation Desert Storm in the Persian Gulf, more missions were flown by F-16s than any other type of airplane.

In the air after the attack, fighter pilots flew in wider and wider circles, keeping watch. An F-16 Fighting Falcon in flight is an incredible sight. On September 11, people near the World Trade Center cheered the flights. The jets made the skies above them safer.

The U.S. Air Force is made up of more than just fighter pilots. Air Force medical teams acted quickly, setting up temporary hospitals. **Medevac** units prepared helicopters to move the wounded to hospitals. With all other airplanes grounded, air force planes delivered more than 1,600 units of blood to New York and Washington.

An army National Guard soldier stands guard as smoke still rises from the World Trade Center a day after the attack.

Into the Wild, Blue Yonder

"Off we go, into the wild blue yonder, flying high into the sun...."
This is the first line of the United States Air Force's official song. It is also the way of life for the 370,000 men and women in the air force.

The U.S. Air Force is the branch of the United States armed forces that is responsible for military action in the sky and space.

The air force is the newest of the U.S. armed forces. The army and the navy have been active for hundreds of years, but airplanes are a recent invention. The first successful airplane flight was in 1903.

Know It

The official U.S. Air Force song was written when the air force was a part of the army. In 1938, there was a contest to find the official song of the Army Air Corps. Of 757 entries, one written by Robert Crawford was chosen by a group of air corps wives. Its original title was "Nothing Will Stop the Army Air Corps." When the air force separated from the Army in 1947, the title changed to "Nothing Will Stop the U.S. Air Force."

Today's air force

Today, the U.S. Air Force has more than 3,500 active aircraft. Fighter and bomber pilots are ready to use these aircraft to defend the United States. These aircraft also support ground troops. The air force uses planes to deliver supplies and more soldiers to those already fighting on the ground or on ships.

The F-16 Fighting Falcon is one of the most advanced jets in the air force.

The Air Force operates this Defense Support Program satellite. This satellite's mission is to "watch" for missiles being launched by enemy forces.

Reconnaissance is a French word meaning recognition. It has come to mean secret observation. Satellites are objects that orbit, or travel around, planets or stars. Moons are natural satellites. Artificial satellites are man-made. U.S. Air Force reconnaissance satellites carry cameras and other equipment. They keep constant watch as they orbit Earth, identifying possible problems.

The air force also invents new equipment for its missions. It has labs and testing centers throughout the United States. Scientists and engineers are among the 170,000 **civilians** who work for the U.S. Air Force.

Some of these scientists work on new technology to keep the country safe from enemies. Other air force scientists forecast weather and track hurricanes. When hurricanes and tornadoes hit communities, the air force helps out.

Air force scientists work with the National Aeronautics and Space Administration (NASA). Air force astronauts have walked in space and piloted space shuttles. NASA and the air force have developed satellites to search for signs of enemy assault. Should an attack seem likely, missiles on the ground are ready to react.

The Army Grows Wings

Before the 1900s, wars were fought on the ground or by sea. A few brave soldiers had climbed into hot air balloons to look over the battlefields below. But their success depended on the wind. Later, dirigibles were used for the same purpose. But their lighter-than-air structure and the flammable gas (gas that will burst into flames) that filled them made them dangerous. To make combat in the sky work, people needed two things: power and wings.

The word *dirigible* comes from the Latin *dirigire*, meaning to steer or direct. Dirigibles are balloons with motors. This makes them easier to steer than balloons. During World War I, dirigibles were used to scout for ships at sea. They were also sometimes used for bombing raids.

On December 17, 1903, the first airplane took off. Wilbur Wright's first flight at Kitty Hawk, North Carolina, lasted only a few seconds. But Wright and others kept making the airplane better. The U.S. Army began to see that the airplane had great possibilities as a weapon.

The Aeronautical Division of the U.S. Army Signal Corps was started on August 1, 1907. There were just three people in it. Their job was to study how the military could use airplanes. In 1911, they dropped the first live bomb from an airplane.

This dirigible, the R34, was built by the British. It was 634 feet (196 meters) long. The R34 was the first dirigible to cross the Atlantic Ocean. The round-trip from Scotland to New York and back to England took almost 8 days.

The very first war airplanes were made from fabric and wire.

In 1915, Dutch-American engineer Anthony Herman Fokker mounted a machine gun with a timing gea on an airplane so that the gun could fire between the plane's rotating propellers.

Know It

In World War I, the Allied forces consisted of 28 countries, including the United States, Great Britain, France, Russia, and Italy. They opposed the Central Powers—Germany, Austria-Hungary, Turkey and Bulgaria.

The first air force

During World War I (1914–1918), designers and engineers built faster and deadlier combat aircraft. The planes were used for **reconnaissance** and for bomb delivery. They raided enemy targets far from the front lines of battle. By the end of the war, the United States had 740 planes, 1,200 pilots, and 200,000 **personnel**. They were called the Air Service, and they helped win the war.

After the war, the government gave the armed forces less money. By June, 1920, the Air Service had only 10,000 personnel. Without money for new planes, they flew dangerous, old aircraft. From July 1920 to July 1921, the Air Service lost 69 pilots in crashes. To get money for new and better planes, they needed to prove that airplanes could be valuable weapons. They had push their airplanes to the limit to show how well they could perform.

An Era of Firsts

Higher. Faster. Farther. U.S. military pilots set out to establish new **altitude,** speed, and distance records. Air Service pilots took part in both military and **civilian** competitions. They did not win them all, but they did win many. These contests allowed them to be the first to accomplish many things.

July 15, 1920

Four Air Service planes left Mitchel Field, Long Island, on a flight from New York to Alaska. They arrived in Nome on August 24, and returned to Long Island on October 20. The 97-day, 9,329-mile (14,970-kilometer) round-trip was an amazing feat in 1920, when pilots had only compasses as tools for **navigation.**

September 4, 1922

Lieutenant Jimmy Doolittle was the first to fly across the United States in a single day. Doolittle took off from Pablo Beach, Florida, and landed at Rockwell Field, near San Diego, California. He made one refueling stop near San Antonio, Texas.

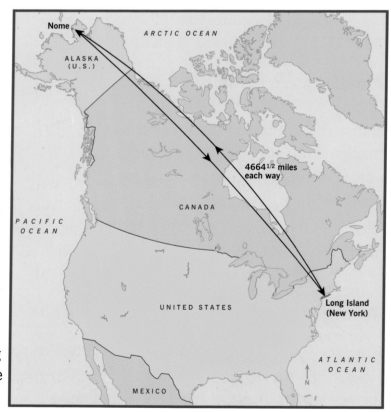

This is the route taken by four Air Service pilots in 1920. Imagine doing this with nothing more than compasses to guide the way!

In 1923, Lieutenants L. H. Smith and J. P. Richter stayed in the air for four days by refueling while airborne.

On May 3 of the following year, Lieutenants John Macready and Oakley Kelly completed the first flight across the country without stopping.

October 25, 1922

Lieutenants L. H. Smith and J. P. Richter refueled a plane in the air for the first time. This allowed airplanes an almost unlimited range.

December 18, 1922

Major Thurman H. Bane piloted the first helicopter to 6 feet (1.8 meters) above the ground. He stayed in the air for 1 minute and 42 seconds.

All of these successful flights showed that aircraft could be useful and perform well for the military. In July 1926, Congress approved a five-year expansion program. It was called the Air Corps Act. It not only changed the name of the air force, but also allowed it to grow. By June 1932, the Air Corps had 1,709 planes and 14,705 **personnel.**

In the 1930s, Air Corps pilots perfected **blind flying**, aerial photography, and airborne communications. To test these new systems, the Air Corps needed new testing grounds. Wright Field, in Dayton, Ohio, opened on October 12, 1927. Engineers and test pilots at Wright worked to make the United States's Air Force the strongest in the world.

The Juggernaut

In March 1935, the War Department established the General Headquarters Air Force. This became the Air Force Combat Command. Its mission was to defend U.S. coastlines from attack by sea. To defend the coasts successfully, the Air Force Combat Command needed a long-range bomber. Later that year, the Boeing Airplane Company produced a four engine, high-speed, long-range bomber called the B-17 Flying Fortress.

Meanwhile, in Germany, Adolf Hitler had come to power in 1933. For six years, he built his forces. On September 1, 1939, Hitler's **juggernaut** invaded Poland, launching World War II. German air power was awesome. Within months it helped Hitler control large areas of Europe.

The United States was not involved in the war, but the armed forces prepared to protect the country. In May 1940, President Franklin D. Roosevelt called for the production of 50,000 military planes a year.

Blitzkrieg means "lightning war." The word is used to describe the way the Germans took over countries in World War II. They used many airplanes to bomb major cities as heavily as possible and then marched into the cities and took power.

The P-51 Mustang is a fighter that was invented for use in World War II.

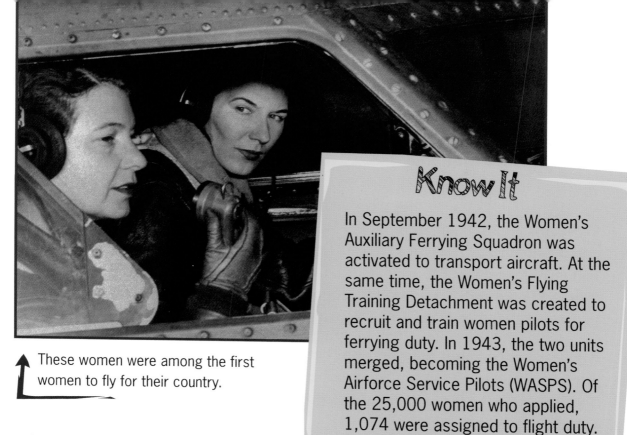

These women were among the first women to fly for their country.

Pilot training programs became more popular. The Air Force Combat Command and the Air Corps merged. They became the Army Air Force.

On December 7, 1941, the Japanese bombed Pearl Harbor, in Hawaii. The United States could no longer avoid the war. When the United States declared war on Germany and Japan, the Army Air Forces had 354,000 men, including 9,000 pilots. But they only had 1,150 combat-ready planes. And the under-equipped American pilots had to fight in two locations, Europe and the lands in the Pacific.

As the war progressed, every Army Air Force pilot was kept busy at the front lines. But pilots were also needed to deliver aircraft, cargo, and passengers. People in the army reserves and **civilians** were trained to fly so they could do these things. When they completed their training, these men were **commissioned** as officers. They were called service pilots.

Eventually, the service pilots were moved to combat duty. When that happened, female pilots took over the service roles.

Mushroom Clouds and Missiles

By May 1945, heavy bombing had helped the Allied forces defeat Germany. Still, the Japanese refused to surrender. In a move both praised and condemned, President Harry S. Truman ordered the use of a secret and terrible weapon. On August 6th, the B-29 bomber *Enola Gay* dropped an **atomic** bomb on Hiroshima, Japan. Three days later, another bomb was dropped on Nagasaki. Japan surrendered on August 14, 1945.

The war was over, but the world was nervous about the United States's power and its atomic bomb. Soon, other countries made atomic bombs. The development of atomic power in the world helped start the **cold war.**

The cold war was not a combat war like World War II. It was a standoff between democratic and **communist** nations. The two sides did not trust each other and that led to conflicts, such as the Korean War and the Vietnam War. As each side built atomic weapons, air power became more important. On July 26, 1947, President Truman signed the National Security Act of 1947. This created an independent United States Air Force for "offensive and defensive air operations."

Following World War II, the army air forces participated in **nuclear** testing. Operation Crossroads was a test conducted at Bikini Atoll, 2,000 miles (3,219 kilometers) southwest of Hawaii. Later, tests were conducted in the Nevada desert.

The U.S. Air Force developed new technologies such as jet aircraft and ground-to-air pilotless aircraft (GAPA). GAPA were missiles that were launched from the ground instead of from an airplane. Flight testing of jets and other experimental aircraft moved to Muroc Field (which was later called Edwards Air Force Base) in California and Wright-Patterson Air Force Base in Ohio.

The Cuban Missile Crisis of 1962 showed the need to spy from the air. The Soviet Union denied having missiles in Cuba, only 90 miles (145 kilometers) from U.S. shores. But photographs from a U-2 spy plane clearly showed Soviet-built missiles being delivered to Cuba. On October 22, President John F. Kennedy announced a naval **blockade** of Cuban waters. Six days later, the Soviets agreed to remove the missiles.

One of the most important missions during the cold war years was electronic and photographic **reconnaissance.** Air force crews often flew close to armed borders or just beyond twelve miles from a country's seacoast, where **international** waters begin.. In addition to spy planes like the U-2, air force researchers developed satellites for spying from space.

GAPA looked like telephone poles with fins attached. The first one was tested in 1946. It was never used as a weapon, but it was a model for later missiles. This GAPA, tested in 1949, reached an altitude of 59,000 feet (almost 18,000 meters).

Global Vigilance

Today the air force is active in three main ways: defense (protection), deterrence (prevention of war), and offense (attack). These three missions are accomplished through the air force's vision of "global **vigilance,** reach, and power." To be vigilant is to be alert.

The power and strength of the air force may serve to prevent a war. An enemy may not want to risk the injuries, death, and property damage that can come from a battle.

Like a good sports team, the air force plays defense. A good defense keeps **civilians** safe from air attacks. **Reconnaissance** satellites patrol the skies. They keep an eye on man-made objects in space and watch for missiles moving toward North American **airspace.**

Ground **radars** in Alaska, Greenland, Massachusetts, Georgia, Texas, and California keep constant watch. The air force also carries radar aboard its Airborne Warning and Control System (AWACS) planes.

Defending the United States

Since the World Trade Center and Pentagon attacks in 2001, there is more focus on **domestic** defense. More than 100 jets, at 26 bases across the country, stand ready to take off on 10 minutes' notice. Before the attacks, only 14 jets at 7 bases were on alert. AWACS have also stepped up domestic patrols.

AWACS planes patrol American skies and can help with U.S. air strikes around the world. The radars and satellites make up an "early warning system." The system is managed by the North American Aerospace Defense Command (NORAD) in Colorado.

NORAD

NORAD is an air warning center, hidden deep within a mountain in Colorado. It is run by the United States and Canada, under the command of the U.S. Air Force. NORAD's basic mission is to keep North American airspace safe from attack by planes, missiles, or space vehicles. Radars on the ground detect these threats. If there is an attack, aircraft or missiles would be sent to destroy the enemy aircraft or missiles. Since the **terrorist** attacks of September 11, 2001, NORAD has changed. Workers are now busy looking for possible threats already inside the United States.

Global Power

The United States Air Force also plays offense in two ways. **Tactical** air attacks target enemy troops and equipment at the front lines of combat. Tactical air units give support to their ground troops and fight for control of the skies above a battle area. **Strategic** air attacks hit far behind the lines. They destroy the enemy's industries and take out bridges, roads, or train tracks that move troops, equipment, and supplies into battle.

The air force has a lot of effective weapons to choose from. The main two types are bombs and missiles. Both can deliver terrible **nuclear** blasts. A gigantic missile can travel 9,200 miles (14,800 kilometers) and destroy an entire city. No country has ever launched such a missile against another nation. But they are important to military planning, and so are called strategic weapons.

Know It

Small bombs can be thrown like grenades, fired from guns, or made to explode with a fuse or timer. Bombs dropped from airplanes weigh from 500 to 15,000 pounds (230 to 680 kilograms). They are considered gravity weapons because Earth's pull brings them toward the ground. Missiles are bomblike weapons that fly under their own power. The part of a missile that explodes is called a warhead.

This is a ballistic missile taking off.

Bombs and missiles

There are many different kinds of bombs:

Incendiary bombs start fires.

Napalm bombs are incendiary bombs (they are meant to start fires) that are filled with jellied gasoline.

Armor-piercing bombs can pierce a ship's armor before exploding.

Cluster bombs have many small bombs, called bomblets, packed in a light container. Once released, the container opens, scattering the bomblets over a wide area.

This laser-guided CBU-87 (Cluster Bomb Unit) is used only by F-117 fighter planes. It can hit a 1-square-yard (0.914-square-meter) target from an altitude of 25,000 feet (7,620 meters).

Guided, or **smart bombs** find their targets with the help of electronic equipment. One kind carries a camera. The pilot looks at the target through the camera and adjusts its path with a remote control. Another kind has a sensing instrument that follows a **laser** beam to its target.

There are different kinds of missiles, too:

Ballistic missiles follow an arching path, like a baseball when it is thrown. A rocket engine blasts a ballistic missile onto a planned course and gives it speed, then shuts off. The missile coasts, then falls on its target.

Nonballistic missiles need a rocket for their entire flight. There are four kinds, depending on where their flight begins and ends. They are surface-to-surface, surface-to-air, air-to-air, and air-to-surface.

Up in the Sky

The F-16 Fighting Falcon is a single-engine fighter plane. It can fly at twice the speed of sound. That is 1,500 miles (2,400 kilometers) per hour)! It can also change direction very quickly. The extreme speed of this plane puts the pilots under great physical stress.

Here is a closer look at some U.S. Air Force aircraft:

B-2 Spirit Stealth bombers and **F-117A Stealth fighters** supply massive firepower. They use stealth, which means they are difficult to "see" by electronic technology such as **radar.**

The U.S. Air Force has named its aircraft with letters and numbers. The letter refers to the mission of the plane: A, attack; B, bomber; C, cargo; F, fighter; H, helicopter; K, tanker; R, **reconnaissance**; T, trainer.

C-130 Hercules and **C-17 Globemaster cargo planes** drop troops, equipment, and other cargo into hostile areas or operating bases.

RQ-1 Predators are unmanned **surveillance** planes that are used in areas that are too dangerous for human pilots to fly over.

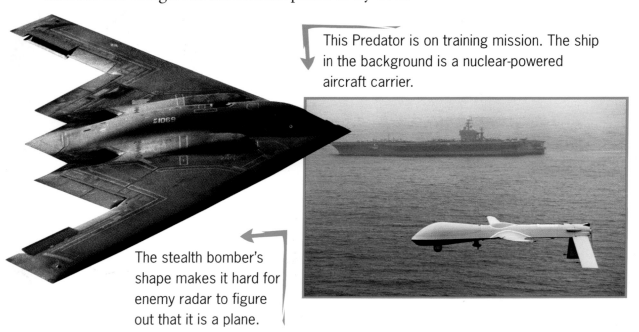

This Predator is on training mission. The ship in the background is a nuclear-powered aircraft carrier.

The stealth bomber's shape makes it hard for enemy radar to figure out that it is a plane.

The B-52 is a long-range bomber.

B-52 Stratofortress and
B-1B Lancer bombers are high
altitude, long-range bombers that
deliver both bombs and missiles.

MH-53J/M-Pave Low and
HH-60G Pave Hawk helicopters
enter enemy territory to recover pilots whose
planes have gone down. They also deliver,
recover, or resupply **special operations forces**.

Air Force One includes two different planes
that are used by the president to travel around
the world.

This Pave Low is a training mission. In front of it is the refueling line from an HC-130 aircraft.

The president and other government officials travel on Air Force One.

Know It

Each flight a combat plane makes against the enemy is called a sortie. An attack by one or more planes is a combat mission. Five planes in a group might fly one combat mission, but five sorties.

UNITED STATES OF AMERICA

28000

Elements and Commands

The commander in chief of the U.S. armed forces is the president of the United States. The president has the final say in all military actions. People who report to the president also make decisions. The Air Force chain of command is

President of the United States
commander in chief

Secretary of Defense
civilian, appointed by the president, who supervises all of the armed forces

Secretary of the Air Force
civilian, responsible for the Department of the Air Force, which includes all parts of the Air Force

Air Force Chief of Staff
a four-star general and one of the Joint Chiefs of Staff. (The other Joint Chiefs are from the Army, Navy, and Marine Corps. They all advise the president).

The Air Force chief of staff and his or her assistants are called **Headquarters Air Force** or the **air staff.**

These are the insignia of the United States Armed Forces. The marine corps (second from top) is part of the navy.

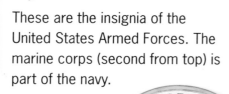

The **air staff** has headquarters in the Pentagon Building near Washington D.C. They oversee nine major commands:

Combat Commands

Combat commands provide combat forces for the fighting missions of the U.S. Air Force. The major commands listed below are divided into smaller units called air forces, wings, and squadrons. A squadron usually has 20 to 25 aircraft. All combat-ready weapons and aircraft of the Air Force belong to one of these commands:

- ⭐ **Air Combat Command,** Langley Air Force Base (AFB), Virginia
- ⭐ **Pacific Air Forces,** Hickam AFB, Hawaii
- ⭐ **United States Air Forces** in Europe, Ramstein Air Base, Germany
- ⭐ **Air Force Special Operations Command,** Hurlburt Field, Florida
- ⭐ **Air Force Space Command,** Peterson AFB, Colorado
- ⭐ **Air Force Reserve Command,** Robins AFB, Georgia

Support Commands

Support commands help the combat commands of all of the armed services:

- ⭐ **Air Mobility Command,** Scott AFB, Illinois, transports troops and supplies and refuels fighters and bombers in air.
- ⭐ **Air Force Materiel Command,** Wright-Patterson AFB, Ohio, buys aircraft, missiles, and supplies.
- ⭐ **Air Education and Training Command,** Randolph AFB, Texas, recruits, trains, and educates U.S. Air Force **personnel.**

The Pentagon, in Washington, D.C., is the headquarters for the U.S. military. There are 17.5 miles (28 kilometers) of hallways in the building.

Joining Up

To join the air force, you must be 17 to 27 years old and have a high school diploma. You must meet height and weight requirements, pass physical and written tests, and be "of good moral character," meaning you do not lie, steal, cheat, hurt others, or use drugs.

Basic Military Training

Once you are in the air force, you must follow orders. Sometimes that means putting your life in danger. With 90 major bases around the world, most air force **personnel** serve some time overseas. But the first place they go to is Lackland AFB, Texas, where they will have six weeks of basic military training, or BMT.

At Lackland, trainees are assigned to a flight. A flight is a group of 45 to 60 people. The group is given a military training instructor, or MTI. It is the MTI's job to make sure that each trainee meets air force standards and performs as part of the team.

This is the High Step obstacle course.

Training begins at 5:00 A.M. every day and ends around 9:00 P.M. Trainees learn whom, when, and how to salute. They also march or run in step with one another. This teaches teamwork.

All trainees do physical conditioning six days a week. This consists of running, stretching, and strength training, including push-ups, sit-ups, and weights. Trainees also spend 40 hours in the classroom. There, they learn about the air force.

The fifth week of basic training is called Warrior Week. The goal is to prepare trainees for combat situations. The trainees spend week five learning basic survival skills. They eat packaged Meals-Ready-to-Eat (MREs) and some hot meals, served in a field **mess** tent. When the week is over, trainees receive an airman's coin and **insignia**. In today's air force, both women and men are called airmen.

Warrior Week

During Warrior Week, air force trainees learn

- how to build defensive fighting positions and put up field tents,
- how to guard against **nuclear, biological,** and chemical attacks,
- emergency first aid, and
- how to guard against **terrorist** threats.

Trainees navigating the obstacle course.

Up Through the Ranks

↑ This F-15 frame was set on fire as a rehearsal for U.S. Air Force fire fighters.

More than 36,000 men and women pass Basic Military Training every year. What happens next depends on whether they are **enlisted** or **commissioned** officers. Enlisted **personnel** go on to technical training in one of 40 career fields. Specialties include aircraft maintenance, medical services, computer systems, security, air traffic control, intelligence, fire fighting, and space and missile operations.

Upon completion of technical training, an airman may choose from eight U.S. and overseas bases where the skills he or she has learned can be used. If one particular base needs more personnel, the airman will be assigned there.

Airmen with higher rank receive higher pay. Someone who joins the air force right out of high school, without any military preparation, is called an airman basic or an E-1.

A commissioned officer holds the rank of second lieutenant or above.

Two ROTC air force cadets in Alaska work with an Airman 1st Class as they learn about an F-15 Eagle.

To join as an E-2, an airman must have taken a few college classes or have two years of Reserve Officer Training Corps (ROTC) or Civil Air Patrol (CAP). A person who has completed more college classes or three years of ROTC can join as an E-3.

After six months, an E-1 who performs well becomes an E-2. After ten more months, he or she may earn the E-3 rank. Twenty months later, or three years total, a person might gain the E-4 rank. After that, moving up in rank requires written and physical fitness tests.

The enlisted rank structure looks like this:

Airman Basic . . . .(E-1)

Airman . . . .(E-2)

Airman First Class . . . .(E-3)

Senior Airman . . . .(E-4)

Staff Sergeant . . . .(E-5)

Technical Sergeant . . . .(E-6)

Master Sergeant . . . .(E-7)

Senior Master Sergeant . . . .(E-8)

Chief Master Sergeant . . . .(E-9)

Chief Master Sergeant of the Air Force . .(E-9)

So You Want to Be a Pilot?

U.S. Air Force pilots must be **commissioned** officers. Commissioned officers need a college degree and officer training. While in college, people who want to be pilots take several tests at Lackland. This allows them to decide whether they really want to fly. And it allows the Air Force to decide if they will make it as pilots.

After finishing college, they become second lieutenants in the Air Force. They are assigned to one of several Undergraduate Pilot Training bases. Training begins with five weeks of classes. Flight training begins in week six. Candidates start by earning their private pilot's license, then learn military flying skills.

They first train in T-37 twin-engine jet trainers. For five months, they have classroom and flight training for twelve hours each day. Then, they move up to T-38 Talon supersonic (faster than the speed of sound) jets.

Pilots in training work at computers that have been set up to show real life situations. The woman is a **civilian** employee who is programming the pilots' terminals to show different problems they might see when flying their planes.

↑ After much hard work, the U. S. Air Force Academy Class of 2002 celebrates its graduation. The Thunderbirds, a demonstration flight team, flies overhead.

Toward the end of their T-38 training, they are ranked on how well they perform. Student pilots then choose one of several advanced "tracks." The best students earn the best tracks, which include fighters and bombers, helicopters, and transport.

The Air Force Academy

Some young men and women choose to attend the United States Air Force Academy. During this four-year program, cadets receive a college education. They graduate with a bachelor of science degree and are **commissioned** as second lieutenants in the air force. Graduates must serve on active duty for at least six years.

Many Air Force pilots begin their careers at the United States Air Force Academy, near Colorado Springs, Colorado. About 1,200 cadets are admitted each year. Candidates must have outstanding academic records and physical ability and do well on admission tests. Only U.S. senators, U.S. congressional representatives, and the president or the vice president of the United States can nominate someone to become a student at the Academy.

Air Combat Command

After training, U.S. Air Force **personnel** with combat-related jobs are assigned to a base under the Air Combat Command (ACC). ACC employs more than 110,000 active duty and **civilian** women and men. There are more than 61,000 men and women in the ACC reserves. ACC aircrews take care of more than 1,700 aircraft.

Organizing the Air Combat Command

Air Combat Command has headquarters at Langley AFB, Virginia. The command's forces are organized into four air force units, one air force reserve unit, and four additional units. They are stationed at sixteen major air bases across the United States. Each conducts specialized operations. For example, the First Air Force unit assists air defense forces that work to protect the United States. The Eighth Air Force supports combat commanders all over the world with strike forces, **surveillance**, and **reconnaissance.**

The Air Force Rescue Coordination Center is also under the Air Combat Command. Located at Langley, it handles all government-ordered search and rescue missions in the United States. It also provides search-and-rescue aid to Mexico and Canada. Since it opened in 1974, the center has saved more than 12,475 lives.

Members of the Pacific Rescue Coordination Center, in Hawaii, drink water from parts of a banana tree during a training drill.

Living on a Base

Langley is one of the largest fighter bases under the Air Combat Command. It covers 2,900 acres and is home to more than 8,800 military and 2,800 civilian personnel. Although some personnel live nearby, most live on the base, which is basically a self-contained city. Their families live there, too. They enjoy benefits like free medical care and tax-free shopping at the commissary, which is a store on the base.

There are schools, libraries, and churches, fitness and recreation centers, a golf course, and a bowling alley. When friends and family visit, they can stay in base lodging and eat in base restaurants. Several times every day, conversation halts as F-15 Eagles take off and land.

U.S. Air Force Master Sergeant Layy Mingus takes a walk with his family and friends on a break from his duties. He lives at Eielson Air Force Base in Alaska.

Fly with Fighter Pilot Doug Larson

Until he reached high school, Major Douglas Larson wanted to be an airline pilot. Then he visited Hill AFB and an F-4 Phantom flew by. He knew immediately that he wanted to be a fighter pilot. "I started asking how I could become a military pilot," he said. "With the help of my mom and some great high school counselors, I received a full scholarship to attend ROTC and the University of Utah. In my junior year, I got my first taste of flying. It fueled my passion to fly fighters."

Larson graduated in 1989. He was **commissioned** as a 2nd lieutenant in the U.S. Air Force and assigned to pilot training. The first five weeks were academics. "We went to class for ten to twelve hours a day. At the sixth week, we started flying the T-37 while continuing classroom learning."

After five months, Larson started flying T-38 supersonic jets. "Toward the end of T-38 training, we were ranked on our performance. It was then we put in our aircraft 'dream sheet.' I graduated at the top of my class and was given my first choice, the F-16 Fighting Falcon. It was one of the most exciting days of my life."

Major Doug Larson stands in front of his two crew chiefs with his Thunderbird plane just before taking off.

A Thunderbird breaks off from the other planes during a move called the line break loop. When the Thunderbirds fly in the famous Thunderbird Diamond formation at 450 miles (726 kilometers) per hour, the planes are only 18 inches 45 centimeters) apart.

Larson has been assigned to bases in Florida, Idaho, and Korea, and is currently at Nellis AFB in Nevada, where he flies with the Thunderbird demonstration team. He said a fighter pilot's typical day "begins around 0700 [7:00 A.M], sometimes earlier. We brief about two hours, then fly a one- to two-hour sortie, consisting of air-to-air and air-to-ground tactics. Then we land and spend a couple of hours discussing the good and bad points of the mission."

Fighter pilots have other duties, such as being flight commanders and weapons officers. "These duties take one to four hours every day," Larson said. "We also try to get to the gym for exercise to help us withstand the rigors [physical stress] of flying a high performance fighter. We hardly ever get time for lunch, so we eat on the run."

How does Larson's family feel about his heavy schedule and the dangers he might face? "Of course, they worry. But they know I am dedicated to my country and keeping it free. They also know that Dad is very good at what he does. U.S. Air Force pilots are the best in the world!"

Air Force Office of Special Investigations

The Air Force Office of Special Investigations (AFOSI) looks into threats and attacks on air force **personnel,** bases, and equipment. It is headquartered at Andrews AFB, Maryland. The OSI has been the U.S. Air Force's major **investigative** service since 1948.

The AFOSI has about 2,475 active, reserve, and **civilian** personnel, including about 1,890 special agents. The AFOSI selects and trains its own agents. Only 230 new agents join the AFOSI each year. Applicants with computer skills or who speak foreign languages are wanted. Those who speak Japanese, Turkish, Korean, and Arabic are needed the most.

Counterintelligence acts against the intelligence (spying) activities of an enemy.

Special Agent Daniel Livingston of the Air Force Office of Special Investigations "lifts" a fingerprint from a compact disk.

Trainees go through a basic training course to learn law, **forensics**, report writing, and interview techniques. Graduate trainees spend a year in the field. If they do well, they go to Washington, D.C., for advanced training. Some agents learn things like photographic and electronic **surveillance**, antiterrorism, and how to use lie detectors.

- The AFOSI was founded in 1948.
- AFOSI's motto is "Eyes of the Eagle."
- Working for the AFOSI is the second most requested career choice in the air force. (Being a pilot is the first choice.)

AFOSI operations

Threat Detection efforts deal with the threat to air force security posed by enemy intelligence services and terrorist groups. Agents investigate **espionage, terrorism,** and technology theft.

Antiterrorism Teams were created to fight worldwide terrorism.

Information Operations investigators respond worldwide to computer hacking into (breaking into using another computer) air force systems.

Technology Protection is necessary because potential enemies often try to steal or copy air force technologies. This program, nicknamed Seven Phoenix, safeguards air force technology, programs, **personnel,** and facilities.

The **Defense Cyber Crime Center** uses computers to process evidence for the Department of Defense.

Specialized Services agents include computer and lie detector experts, behavioral scientists, and forensic advisors.

Criminal Investigations investigate crimes committed within the air force, including robbery, assault, burglaries, drug dealing, and **fraud.**

A Day with the AFOSI

Most bases have only 3 or 4 AFOSI investigators. But at Nellis AFB, in Nevada, there are 10 investigators. Special Agent Kirk Stabler is their commander. "Nellis is special for a couple of reasons," he said. "It's the home of the Thunderbirds, which means we get a lot of people through here, wanting to watch them practice. And Las Vegas is a high-crime city."

On the job with AFOSI

When air force **personnel** are involved in crimes, on base or off, the AFOSI investigates. Many crimes involve drugs. The air force maintains zero tolerance for drugs. "You wouldn't want a pilot flying while on drugs," said Stabler. "And you wouldn't want a jet mechanic to do his job while under the influence. Our whole focus is keeping American warfighters safe."

Airman 1st Class Allison Vasey, an Intelligence Operations Specialist for the Office of Special Investigations, talks to an aircraft commander (center) about the runway at Kigali, Rwanda, before a mission begins.

Thousands of people come to Nellis AFB to see the Thunderbirds perform. Here, the team flies F-16 Fighting Falcons in a delta formation during training.

At Nellis, Steven Lewis is the senior special agent in charge of day-to-day operations. Like most members of his crime team, Lewis enlisted in the air force. Later, he "cross-trained" into the AFOSI. "I'd always had an interest in criminology," [the study of crime] he said. "The Air Force helped me earn my degree in criminal justice and assigned me here."

Besides keeping track of drug, assault, and **fraud** investigations, Lewis works with new agents. The new agents spend a year in on-the-job training to make sure they are good enough for the AFOSI.

Another person assigned to Nellis AFB is Captain Adrienne Pederson, an ROTC graduate. She began her air force career as an information management specialist. After assignments in Germany and Texas, she trained for the AFOSI. "I wanted a challenge," she explained, "and after September 11, I got it." Pederson was invited to join a **terrorism** task force. She works with the Federal Bureau of Investigation, the Department of Alcohol, Tobacco, and Firearms, the Federal Aviation Administration, and Las Vegas law enforcement. "We investigate any threat of terrorism, from anthrax to bomb scares."

Air Force Research Laboratory

The Air Force Research Laboratory (AFRL) is always looking for and developing the newest technologies. Of 5,400 people working for the AFRL, 4,100 are **civilians.** Nearly 80 percent of the research takes place at universities or within U.S. industries. They look at the latest aircraft, space vehicles, rockets, weapons, lasers, microwaves, and fuels.

The B-2 Spirit Stealth bomber is a good example of a technology that was developed by the AFRL and private businesses working together. Research into how to make a plane difficult for the enemy to find led to the plane's design. Its materials and its shape make it difficult for **radar** and other systems to find it when it is flying.

The B-2 Spirit Stealth bomber does not look like a plane to human eyes. It also doesn't "look" like a plane to enemy radar because it isn't made of the same kinds of materials as a regular plane.

The first flight of a B-2 Stealth bomber took place on July 17, 1989. All B-2 Stealth planes are flight tested at Edwards AFB, California. Then, they go to Whiteman AFB, Missouri, which is the base that B-2 Stealths operate from.

High-power microwaves make it possible to destroy electronic enemy weapon systems without putting soldiers in danger. A microwave in a home usually has no more than 1,500 watts of power. A military high-power microwave can produce millions of watts. When it is aimed at a weapons system, it causes the system to "burn out" and stop working.

Nonweapon research

Not all the research at the AFRL is on weapons. The Laser Medical Pen can be used by doctors on the battlefield to treat wounded soldiers. It can cut like a scalpel (knife) and can stop a wound from bleeding. It can also sterilize, or clean, a wound to help prevent infection. The Laser Medical Pen runs on batteries, is 12 inches (20 centimeters) long, less than 1 inch (2 1/2 centimeters) thick, and weighs only 1 pound (almost 1/2 kilogram).

The Laser Medical Pen, or Medpen, runs on batteries. It can clean a wound by sterilizing it and then close the wound. It can also cut like a surgeon's scalpel.

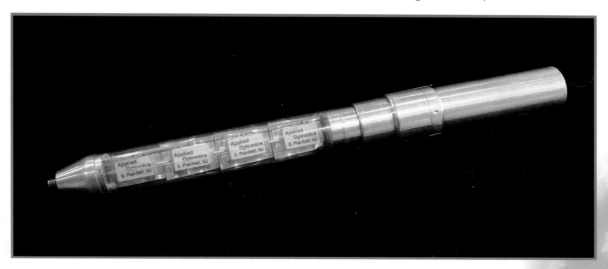

Air National Guard and Air Force Reserves

We are most familiar with members of the U.S. Air Force who are on active duty all the time. They may live on bases in the United States or other countries. But there are others in the air force who go to work in times of war and national emergencies. They are the Air National Guard and the Air Force Reserves. These people have several missions.

There are 107,000 men and women in the Air National Guard. They provide almost half the U.S. Air Force's airlift support, combat **communications**, medical evacuations, and aerial refueling. They are also responsible for the air defense of the entire United States.

Air National Guard units are in each state. When not on federal duty, Air National Guard units can be called on by the states' governors. They do search-and-rescue missions, emergency relief during natural disasters, and antidrug operations.

Reservists move a barrier into position during Operation Enduring Freedom.

A C-130 Hercules used by the Air Force Reserve dumps chemicals over a forest to protect it from burning during the dry season.

The Air Force Reserve Command has more than 193,000 trained reservists. They may be called to active duty in time of war or national emergencies. Some reservists train on a regular schedule. They are members of the Select Reserve. These reservists are always ready for duty and can be sent anywhere in the world within 72 hours.

Today, many air force reservists are on duty all around the world. In addition to combat missions, Air Force Reserve **personnel** conduct **humanitarian** relief missions. That could mean building roads and schools or airlifting supplies to victims of floods and earthquakes. Using specially equipped C-130s, reservists also fight forest fires and oil spills.

Air Force Space Command

In 1957, the Soviet Union launched the first successful satellite. It was called Sputnik I. The satellite was sent into space by an **intercontinental** ballistic missile (ICBM). This type of missile could reach military targets in less than an hour, something no bomber could do. The United States saw the need to get this kind of power, and the U.S. military expanded their activities to include space.

Outer space is the best place from which to see what is happening all over Earth. Satellites can send weather information and missile warnings, provide communication links, help with **navigation,** and supply intelligence. The satellite systems that perform

Know It

The Air Force Space Command has four main mission areas:
- *Space forces support* launches satellites into space and operates them once they are there.
- *Space control* maintains friendly use of outer space through **surveillance.**
- *Force enhancement* provides weather data, communications, intelligence, missile warning, and **navigation.**
- *Force application* maintains and operates a land-based ICBM force.

This Air Force Space Command worker is in an underground bunker of a missile command center that is no longer used.

these duties are run by the Air Force Space Command (AFSPC). The command's mission is to make sure the United States will always have access to space and to maintain the country's land-based ICBMs.

The U.S. military worked on space missions for many years before the Air Force Space Command was established in 1982. Its headquarters are at Peterson AFB in Colorado. About 40,000 people work on the command's missions.

The Air Force Space Command keeps 500 missiles on constant alert. This is how the air force deters, or prevents war.

U.S. space forces are always watching what is happening around the world. Often, they are the first to spot possible problems. Sometimes this allows nations to settle their conflicts without fighting. But when war is waged, information gathered from space gives the United States and its allies an advantage.

A Minuteman III intercontinental ballistic missile is launched.

Some 10,000 known objects are orbiting Earth right now. These range from satellites to space junk that comes from launches. The U.S. Space Command's Space Control Center keeps track of these objects.

43

Air Force Vision

The U.S. Air Force has changed greatly since it was started in the early 1900s. From those first planes and wobbly helicopters, it has grown into a large, strong fighting force. And it is no longer just an air force, but a space force, too.

When the **cold war** ended, old enemies became allies. But new enemies can be hard to identify. Warfare has changed. Fighting uses fewer bullets and more careful planning. The U.S. Air Force has changed along with the world. Space technology has become more important. To remain a leader in space warfare, the U.S. Air Force started the Space Battlelab in 1997. The battlelab develops new ideas and judges whether they will work. Those that do work are quickly put to use.

The youngest branch of the military will continue to answer the new challenges.

Airman Basic Amy Ting is one person who answered the new challenges. She escaped from a hotel in the World Trade Center on September 11, 2001, just before it fell down. She decided to give up her career as an actress and joined the air force. She completed her basic training at Lackland AFB in Texas.

Global
Vigilance
Reach &
Power

America's Air Force

Looking toward the future

The United States Air Force has focused on the future with its Global Vigilance, Reach and Power program. This is the air force part of the military's Vision 2020 program. Some of the air forces mission statements include:

- recruit, train, and retain America's best young men and women to provide **global** vigilance, reach, and power into the 21st Century;

- size, shape, and operate the force to meet the needs of the nation;

- continue to combine air, space, and information operations;

- continue exploring both science and technology;

- continue integrating air, space, and information operations;

- continue to develop leaders who can use the forces to accomplish these goals.

Glossary

acoustic having to do with sound

airspace space in the air above a section of the earth

altitude height

biological having to do with living organisms, such as bacteria

blind flying flying without seeing outside of the airplane, using only instruments

blockade control of what goes in or out of a place, especially by armed forces

civilian anyone not in the armed forces

cold war disagreements between the United States and countries that used to be communist .It lasted for years. They continued to communicate, however, and did not fight war with weapons.

commissioned given rank by a written order

communications sharing information

communist a person or country which supports communism. Communism is a system where most property is owned by the state and is supposed to be shared by all.

domestic of one's own country; not foreign

enlisted signed up to be part of the armed forces

espionage spying

forensics the science that applies medical knowledge to questions of law

fraud an activity, that is against the law, performed in order to gain a benefit such as money

global spread throughout the world

humanitarian helpful to people

insignia a medal or badge showing an honor or military rank

intercontinental from one continent to another

international between nations

investigative having to do with careful examination or a detailed search

juggernaut a machine or force that destroys everything in its path

laser a light beam that uses invisible, or infrared light waves

Medevac teams of people, including doctors and nurses, that use helcipoters and planes to remove the wounded

mess a group of people who take meals together, especially armed forces **personnel**

mushroom clouds **mushroom**-shaped clouds of radioactive matter that rises from the explosion of a **nuclear** bomb

navigation the science of figuring out the position of an airplane or ship

nuclear having to do with atomic energy

personnel the people employed in any work, business or service

radar system that uses radio waves to find objects

reconnaissance secret observation of activities

special operations forces branches of the military that undergo special training and operate apart from the regular armed forces

strategy/strategic plan

surveillance watching and listening

terrorist person who uses violence and fear to get something

More Books to Read

Alagna, Magdalena. *Life Inside the Air Force Academy.* Danbury, Conn.: Children's Press, 2002.

Green, Michael. *The United States Air Force.* Mankato, Minn.: Capstone Press, 1998.

Kennedy, Robert C. *Life as an Air Force Fighter Pilot.* Danbury, Conn.: Children's Press, 2000.

Langley, Wanda. *The Air Force in Action.* Berkeley Heights, N.J.: Enslow Publishers, Inc., 2001

Sievert, Terri, et al. *The U.S. Air Force at War.* Mankato, Minn.: Capstone Press, 2001.

Index